T0158791

DANCE ME BEAUTIFUL

DANCE ME BEAUTIFUL

Deborah Graham

iUniverse, Inc.
Bloomington

Dance Me Beautiful

iUniverse books may be ordered through booksellers or by contacting:

iUniverse
1663 Liberty Drive
Bloomington, IN 47403
www.iuniverse.com
1-800-Authors (1-800-288-4677)

ISBN: 978-1-4759-3387-1 (sc)
ISBN: 978-1-4759-3389-5 (e)

Printed in the United States of America

iUniverse rev. date: 07/27/2012

To Christopher, for making every day beautiful.

He leaned forward and kissed her
and she awoke from her long sleep.

—Sleeping Beauty

CONTENTS

INTRODUCTION

Prior to my divorce at age 33, I was living what I thought was an uncomplicated and fortunate life. I grew up with my Mom, Dad and brother in a nice house in a nice neighbourhood. I was a straight-A student who never got into any trouble. I graduated from law school and articled at one of the top firms on Bay Street. I married my high school sweetheart and we bought a lovely house in a small Ontario town. We had a dog and planned to have children. I had my own family law practice on the main street of town.

All was as I had hoped and imagined my life would be.

And then, my marriage crumbled and ended.

As a divorce lawyer, I knew what needed to be done legally, but I had no idea how to emotionally survive a divorce.

When my marriage ended, I grieved it all. I grieved the loss of my marriage, the loss of my hopes, the loss of my dreams and the loss of my innocence. I grieved the broken promises, my broken life and my broken heart.

Why me? I asked over and over until I finally stopped asking.

In one of my darkest, saddest moments, I walked into the Newman Centre (a little church on the University of Toronto campus). I had never been in the church, but a friend of mine played the piano there from time to time. It was a few weeks before Christmas, almost a year after my marriage had ended. The church service was a candlelight advent service. Alone in the very back row, feeling the weight of all of my despair, I came across a quote from Martin Luther King written on the back of the church bulletin,

"Only in the darkness can you see the stars."

All of the lights were off in the church and each of us held an unlit candle. The priest lit the first candle and used its flame to light another and then, one by one, each person shared the flame until every candle was glowing.

"Only in the darkness can you see the stars."

I was inspired by the words of Martin Luther King and the simple ritual I had participated in. Only when the darkness of night descends do the stars become visible. They are the gifts of the night.

I had been weighed down by the darkness of my life and in that moment, I was inspired to look for the stars—the gifts in the darkness. And slowly I began to find them. I received some counselling. I read some helpful books. I kept a gratitude journal and began to appreciate the good in my life and somehow that made the good start to grow. I returned to writing. I created visions of my future and started to hope again.

I began to dance and that is where this story begins.

DANCE ME BEAUTIFUL

"Dance me beautiful," was all I could say. The lump in my throat and the tears welling in my eyes stopped me from saying more. There really wasn't anything else to say.

I remembered riding my horse in the indoor arena one day last winter. I hadn't been riding well, and my horse was not being particularly responsive. As I rode by one of the mirrors, I looked at my reflection and found myself saying, "Ugly." I never even realized what I had said to myself until I was halfway around the arena. It suddenly hit me, and I was furious. I turned my horse around and rode back to that mirror and looked at my reflection. I forced a smile and tried to look at the image staring back at me with kinder, gentler eyes.

When I continued my ride, I was riding from a different place inside. My horse was attentive and responsive, and we moved through our figures as one. I hadn't noticed that several people had entered the arena. We did a spectacular line of flying changes across the diagonal, and I halted and leaned forward to hug my horse around the neck when I heard the clapping and realized we had an audience. Once I started riding from a place of self-love, everything changed and my horse and I were able to work as one.

So when this man asked me what I wanted from dance, the answer was simple. I wanted every ounce of me to feel truly beautiful. I had been dancing for months and finally knew what I wanted.

THE FIRST LESSON

The first time I was introduced to him, he had simply reached out his hand, smiled and said, "Dance with me."

It was such a simple request, such a modest invitation. I stood hesitantly and took a step toward him. I had come here to learn to dance, so why was I so reluctant to begin? Maybe it had been foolish; maybe it had been a mistake. Why had I come? I felt a sickening wave of shame. I felt pathetic. I was 33, divorced and about to pay someone to teach me how to dance. How childish; how frivolous; how foolish. Was I the prototypical lonely and sexually starved divorcee? Was I here to learn how to dance, or was I here to be held? Had I hired a dance instructor or some kind of prostitute?

In response to my hesitation, he asked, "What are you missing in your life that you hope to get from dance?"

"Passion," I heard myself answer. "I want to feel passionate."

Where had those words come from? Is that what I was

looking for? I thought I just wanted to learn how to dance. I couldn't believe I had just told a total stranger that I was looking for passion. Was that not admitting that I was lacking passion in my life? Would he think I meant I wanted sex? Could I take it back? No, I was stuck with it out there. For better or for worse, this man now knew that my life was lacking passion, and I was stuck with that. That was enough for me for one day. I was ready to go home and maybe never come back again.

Instead, I found myself being placed in a dance position. Without saying a word, he placed my left hand on his arm just beneath his shoulder. He placed his right hand on my left shoulder blade and raised his elbow so that my arm was lightly resting on his. He then took my right hand in his left hand and held it up in a traditional dance frame. Somehow it felt like an important moment. I guess in a way it was a moment of small surrender. I was allowing this man to teach me.

Thus began my first dance lesson.

FOLLOWING

He explained to me that he, as the man, would ask me to go somewhere or do something—in other words, lead. I, as the woman, would accept his lead and go where he asked—in other words, I would follow. It sounded simple, but following would turn out to be more complicated than that.

If you lead I shall follow, but only after I have learned and chosen to trust you, and only if your lead is respectful and if I let go and am here in the moment with you.

I thought of my many years as a rider. It was my horse who followed my lead, doing as I bid. The element of trust in the relationship between horse and rider had always struck a chord of sadness in me. I remember hearing that the ultimate test of the training of a dressage horse was for him to jump a fence in front of him even if he had never jumped a fence before, simply because his rider had asked him to go forward in a straight line and the fence was in that straight line. The horse had to trust the rider and he had to trust himself.

I thought of Cindy Ishoy and Dynasty in the moment before she rode Dynasty into the Olympic ring for his medal-winning performance. She'd had to ride him through a tunnel into the stadium. The tunnel was vibrating from the stomping of the spectators above. Dynasty had never encountered anything like this before. She felt his fear as his heart pounded between her legs and sweat broke out on his neck. She felt every muscle in his body ready to turn and run. He needed to respond to the flight instinct developed over thousands and thousands of years. She squeezed her legs and asked him to go forward, and with barely a moment's hesitation, he did. His trust in her overcame his every instinct, his very evolution. She was so proud of him and was so moved by his absolute trust in her that she no longer cared what happened in the ring. She and her horse had just shared their most important Olympic memory. Even though they went on to have the ride of a lifetime and helped win the first medal ever for a Canadian dressage team, it is the moment in the tunnel that she talks most about, and it is the moment in the tunnel that touches me somewhere deep inside.

It is an incredible responsibility to be absolutely trusted, and I had always tried to respect that, never asking my horse for more than I knew he could give.

But now I was not being given someone's trust. I was the one being asked to trust. I was being asked to follow. Would I accept? This man had something I wanted and the only way for me to get it was to trust him.

But how many times was I to trust, only to be disappointed?

How many hurts can a heart withstand before it gives up? I needed to know more about this man asking me to follow. I would go slow.

THE DANCE FRAME

"Look up to the heavens and open your heart to receive joy," he said as he encouraged me to hold my frame even when it felt physically and emotionally unbearable. He supported my spine with his hands and supported my heart with his soothing presence. "Whatever you are feeling, whatever you are experiencing, just stay with it."

I did not know what I was experiencing but knew that I did not want to stay with it. I was leaning back, looking up and out, and somehow that was incredibly uncomfortable and made me want to cry. I was experiencing something unfamiliar and uncomfortable, and I felt extraordinarily self-conscious. But it also felt intriguing and inviting. I did not want to stay there any longer, but I somehow sensed that I might want to return.

He stayed with me through the worst of it. I relaxed into it and then he commented on the beautiful flush that had come over me. Suddenly I felt that I had been caught smiling at my reflection in the mirror and I was embarrassed.

Days later I realized that this dance frame, in which my chest opens outward and upward and where my head and heart lift up to the heavens, is the exact opposite of shame. It's like saying, "Hello, world, I'm here and I have a right to be here, and I'm not going anywhere!" It's a moment of unabashedly smiling at oneself. It's being vulnerable and powerful at the same time. It's a moment of surrender and acceptance and of letting go. It's peace and stillness, movement and freedom.

JOIN UP

In dance competitions the etiquette is for the man and woman to stand 10 feet apart and for the man to hold his left hand out in dance position, thus inviting the woman to dance. The woman then walks toward the man with an attitude of acceptance and confidence and joins the man in the dance frame.

Standing 10 feet from my dance instructor and seeing him invite me to dance left me immobilized. I did not want to go to him; I wanted him to come to me. It was as if I did not want him to know that I wanted to dance with him enough to walk those 10 feet to join him. I realized that I feared being mocked for wanting to join him, for wanting to be with him, for needing something from him.

I had a dream the other night in which I was a young child and was running through the forest. I was running away as fast and as far as I could. I finally stopped and sat down leaning against a tree with my arms around my knees. I started to cry. I was lost and lonely and frightened. I had run too far for anyone to come and find me. And I had no one to blame but myself. I had run away but I wanted—needed—someone to run after me, to come and find me. I felt sad to my very core. I felt as if I would just stay there by myself, forever.

This "join up" was going to be important for me. This was the moment in which I would have to pick myself up and start walking out of the forest. It was going to be a moment when I stopped playing hide-and-seek and stepped forward to be counted.

It would be a while before I could walk toward this man and join him.

The next time he stood away from me and invited me to dance, I found myself circling him and was reminded of Monty Roberts, the real-life "horse whisperer." Instead of "breaking" young horses, his methods are based on the language of a flight animal and the advance/retreat instinct. He earns the trust of a young, unhandled horse by speaking its language. When the horse is first introduced into the ring where Monty is standing, it is afraid and wants to be as far away from Monty as possible. The horse is a flight animal, and Monty is a fight animal.

Monty accepts the horse's need to run away and even encourages it by advancing toward the horse. This continues until the horse drops its head and starts to "chew" (letting Monty know it wants to renegotiate). Monty then retreats, or turns away from the horse, letting the horse know that he will not harm it and that he understands its language. By turning away, Monty invites the horse in. Invariably, the horse will turn in and walk toward Monty. The horse approaches Monty cautiously but voluntarily. The horse is, in effect, taking a leap of faith.

There is this beautiful moment called "join up" when the horse reaches Monty and Monty strokes it and welcomes it. The moment brings tears to the eyes of all who are watching. The horse easily accepts a saddle being placed on its back and quietly allows Monty to mount it.

I felt a strong connection between the horse choosing to trust Monty and going toward him and my choosing to trust my dance instructor and walking those 10 feet toward him.

YOU HAVE TO BELIEVE IT TO SEE IT

"There's something holding you back, and I can't quite put my finger on it," he said as we stopped dancing and he let go of me.

I stared blankly. I hated when he let go of me. I thought things were going well, but now I felt a sense of failure. I wanted to be a good student and earn praise from the teacher. I had always been a good student. I could quickly determine what was expected of me and then hand it over on a silver platter. If a professor was looking for independent thinking, I would incorporate controversial opinions in my paper. If a professor was looking for his ego stroked, I would feed him back his own views.

My head raced as I tried to figure out what I was missing and quickly assess what this dance teacher was looking for.

He shook his head in confusion and discouragement, and we began to dance again. As we moved across the dance floor, he suddenly asked me, "Do you believe you deserve to dance well?"

I was the one to stop and let go this time. He had caught me completely off guard. I stared at him, at first unable to answer. My eyes filled with tears as I shook my head and responded, "I don't know."

Ever so quietly and gently, he said, "Until you believe you deserve to dance well, until you believe you deserve all the joy that dance has to offer, you will be stuck in the patterns of the dance. You will not experience the dance. You will not dance with passion."

I was suddenly furious. Who did this man think he was? Then I was angry at myself. Why shouldn't I believe I deserve to dance well? What was that about, and why was it coming up in this little dance studio above the chesterfield shop? This man had walked right inside me through the independent barrier, through the lawyer barrier, and through the calm, cool and collected barrier in a matter of seconds.

THE TANGO

I told him I wanted him to teach me the tango. He said yes but then asked why, and I suddenly wished I hadn't asked. I didn't know why I wanted to learn the tango, and I was somehow embarrassed that I had asked. Maybe it was inappropriate for me to learn the tango at this stage. Maybe it was too advanced and I was not ready. I had asked this man for something and maybe he was going to say no, and that seemed like too big a deal. Maybe I needed to change dance instructors. Instead, I simply said, "I want the intensity of the tango."

When I arrived for my next lesson, there was tango music playing and I was grateful that he had not forgotten, that I didn't have to ask again (because I knew I wouldn't) and that he wasn't going to question me further as to why. By the end of that lesson we both knew why I needed to learn the tango. The intensity, aggression, violence and danger of the tango were the places I needed to go to find the passion in my dance and the passion in my life. The waltz and foxtrot felt smooth and safe. I could be romantic and loving and graceful. There was something safe and controlled about the waltz and the foxtrot that mirrored my life. There was nothing about the tango that mirrored my life. The tango would take me places unknown or long forgotten.

He led me through the basic moves of the tango. The lead was powerful, aggressive, almost violent. I did not know where I was going next. There was nothing predictable about this dance. The lead was so strong that there was not a lot of choice about following. I lost myself in the moment and surrendered to the power of the dance—and then something inside of me froze.

It was as if minute fragments of a distant memory flashed throughout my body. I had never experienced anything like this before. I had always experienced the world visually and interpreted the world cognitively. This was some deeper, truer way of experiencing the world, without the distortion of rational or irrational thinking. There was some deep, intrinsic truth stored in my body that I had long forgotten. I had learned to interpret the world through my mind as a young child and had completely lost the part of me that could interpret the world through my body and my senses. It was as if some integral part of being human had returned to me for a brief moment.

I was a bit shaken by the experience, but I felt more alive than I had ever remembered. It was late when I left the studio, but I was not ready to be indoors. I walked under the stars late into the night without fear. I felt powerful and invincible. I felt somehow connected with the universe. I felt larger than life. *Or maybe this was simply what life felt like.*

When I returned home, the power left me and I became afraid. I lay in bed unable to sleep and barely able to breathe. Every sound took my breath away and left me with a feeling of anxious dread. The night was suddenly ominous, and I felt small, disconnected, afraid, helpless and alone.

What the hell had happened in the tango?

Did I dare go back?

I remembered him asking me if I dared live life with the kind of intensity of the tango. He said that most people would rather die than open themselves up to that amount of energy.

I summoned the courage to show up for my next lesson. I think it was curiosity more than anything that brought me back.

I was leaning against the window when he came into the room, and I could not go to him. He came to me and took my hand, but I could not take my back away from the cold, hard glass. It was as if, when I left the security of the glass, I would lose my connection to the cold, hard reality, and I might get lost in that strange world the tango would bring me to.

I looked into the eyes of this man and realized I trusted him. It hadn't been a conscious choice; it had sneaked up on me. He seemed to sense that the window was my lifeline, and he did not pull me away from it. Instead he took my hand, looked right into my eyes and asked if it had been hard for me to come tonight. I nodded. I felt as if I tried to say a word I would crumple on the spot, physically and emotionally, and that maybe I would never be able to pick myself up again. He asked why I had come, and I found myself saying I felt as if there were not a strong cell, muscle or bone in my body and that I wanted to feel strong.

He closed his eyes and took a deep breath. He had a way of doing that. It was as if he could breathe into every part of himself. I envied that. When he opened his eyes, it was as if he had opened his very core, his soul to me. He invited me to find in him what I needed and to take it. It was a generous gift. I sensed that although part of him knew he had enough to give me, part of him feared he didn't, and that my taking it from him would leave him with less.

I took him up on his offer. I looked into his soul and found what I needed. I was careful to take only what I needed. I wanted to stroke his face and tell him he was kind and good.

To this day I don't know what it was that I found in him or how I knew it when I found it. I was learning that things could be real and true even if I did not understand them.

We began to dance. We were connected through trust and love. As we moved across the dance floor I felt the energy flowing through me and felt strong and unafraid. I was able to throw my head back and laugh at the sheer joy of feeling unafraid.

It was hard not to see him the next day.

THE SCHOOL FIGURES

The one thing I hated about my dance lessons was when I had to do school figures. By myself I had to go through each of the five steps I had learned for each dance. I felt incredibly self-conscious and exposed.

Last night, toward the end of the lesson, he took a few steps away from me and asked me to do the basic rumba steps. I quickly went through them with my arms twisted in front of me and my body slouched. He asked me to do it again and put some sex into it. I stood immobilized and then took a few steps toward him and started to cry. I felt small and insignificant and scared and ugly. I did not want to be me.

My arms hung at my sides, and I felt him place his hands over mine. I was looking down and tapping my foot in frustration and in response to my need to run away. And then I felt him ever so softly, ever so gently kiss the top of my head. It was so soft and warm and caring and loving and simple. I melted.

He quietly led me through the steps again and then gently

asked me to do them on my own. I wouldn't. I wasn't ready to let go. I needed his touch, even if it was just the tips of his fingers on mine. He stayed with me as I danced the figures with just the tips of our fingers touching. I would not look away from his eyes. I needed him to be right there with me, body and soul, and I needed to be sure he wasn't leaving.

I felt like when I was a little girl riding my bike without training wheels for the first time, knowing my dad was holding on and how I kept asking him if he was still holding on and kept telling him not to let go. When I discovered that he had let go, part of me was proud that I had been riding my bike on my own and part of me was hurt that he had let go when I had asked him not to.

Here I was, a grown woman learning to dance, and I wanted my dance instructor's reassurance that he would not let go. I decided to trust him and keep quiet. He did not let me down. I began to feel beautiful, and I began to feel sexy. I smiled, and he smiled back.

JOIN UP (AGAIN), OR THE LITTLE GIRL IN ME

He stepped away from me and stood in the "invitation to dance" position. I looked into his eyes and found the acceptance and reassurance I needed. I walked confidently toward him and joined him in the dance position, quite proud of myself for having overcome my earlier reluctance for this join up.

"Good," he said. "Now bring something of yourself to me."

Suddenly I felt like a shy little girl and I scrunched my face into a little girl smile.

"Come now," he said, "bring that with you."

I approached him shyly and quickly. Why did I suddenly feel so awkward? How did this man have the ability to constantly challenge me? Anyone would describe me as self-confident, bright, mature and competent, yet this man could so easily bring me to the little girl inside.

I had once read about meeting your inner child through meditation. It was an opportunity to heal the wounds of your childhood by going back as an adult and kissing them better. I decided to try it. I found myself in my bedroom as it was when I was 5 or 6 years old. I had forgotten that it once had hardwood floors. There I was, a little girl asleep in her bed. I was overcome with love and nostalgia for this little girl. It felt like a reunion with a long-lost love, and I felt joy and sadness mingled as one. I did not want to wake this little girl and wanted to be near her. I quietly lay down beside her. She woke, and she turned around, patted me on the shoulder and said, "Don't worry, everything will be okay." I had expected to go back and comfort the child, but instead she comforted me. She seemed to have more to give me than I had to give her.

Now here was this man awakening that little girl and bringing her forward over and over again. She knew how to dance, she knew how to hold her hands out wide and twirl, she knew how to trust and she knew how to be spontaneous, and this man was inviting her to teach me.

BACK TO THE TANGO, OR THE WOMAN IN ME

I wanted to scream. I wanted to stomp my feet, clamp my hands over my ears and scream. I wanted to shut out the entire world, including myself.

We were facing each other, paused in the tango, when he asked me to show him the woman in me. I stared at him, furious. I knew what he wanted. But I couldn't do it. I couldn't let the woman in me out. I hated him at that moment. And I hated myself. I glared at him, debating whether to stay or go. I knew that if I walked out at that moment, I would never come back. That was tempting, but something inside me refused to leave. And so I just stood there.

I was just beginning to be able to let the little girl out, but now he was asking the woman in me to come out. She felt far too powerful to let loose on this world. She scared me. It was as if being her meant anything was possible. She was confident, sensual and powerful. And I wasn't supposed to be any of those things. In fact, I wasn't supposed to be her.

I left the studio after my lesson that night feeling hopeless and defeated. I did not believe I was capable of rising to the challenge. And if I couldn't rise to the challenge, what was the point?

It was as if my spirit—my life force—was trapped in this body and mind, paralyzed with shame. I was tired of holding back. I wanted to break free but I couldn't. Over the next few days, I felt this energy building and swirling around inside me, looking for places to escape. It was getting harder and harder to contain it. And there was less and less of me wanting to.

I woke from a dream filled with butterflies and was reminded of the day that a butterfly had come to me while riding. I had been riding my horse through the woods when I was overcome with a desire for danger and speed. It was as if I needed to feel fear in order to feel alive. I urged my horse into a canter, and he seemed to sense my need as he broke into a full gallop. We were flying through the woods. The path was twisted and narrow. A voice inside me said to slow down; this was dangerous. I wasn't wearing a helmet and if my horse lost his footing I could be killed. I didn't care. I leaned forward, lowered my body and pressed my face against his neck, partly to protect myself from the low-hanging branches and partly to connect with this muscular, powerful racing horse. I heard the thunder of his hooves, I felt the wind in my face, and I felt the heat of his body. I became one with this horse of mine whose body and soul were racing for the sheer love of running—for the sheer love of his own strength and power. I felt alive.

We burst out of the woods into a peaceful meadow. My

horse slowed to a halt, and we stood breathing heavily, the adrenaline coursing through our bodies. A butterfly came to rest on his neck. I looked at the butterfly and started to cry. I did not understand it at the time but knew that the butterfly was some kind of sign. The butterfly stayed on his neck for the remainder of our walk back to the stable and then flew away.

In many ways this journey resembled the evolution of a butterfly. In a sense, I had created a cocoon, which had felt safe at first. But now it was feeling small and cramped, restricted and claustrophobic. I thought of the butterfly trapped in the cocoon and the energy and fighting that was necessary to destroy the cocoon and break free.

That's exactly where I was. I was tired of the cocoon and needed to physically and emotionally break free. I would need this anger, this energy that was building inside me to break out of my cocoon.

I was ready to fly. I was ready to race through the woods for the sheer love of my own strength and power.

A MOMENT OF DEFEAT

"Thank you for your patience," I said as I was leaving the studio. I was in tears before I even reached my car. What I had really wanted to say was, "Please don't give up on me."

I was tired, disappointed and felt defeated. I had been so excited to break free, and it hadn't happened. For the first time since I started to dance, I was ready to give up.

I came home and went to bed. The tears streamed down my cheeks. I had wanted to ask him if he was ready to give up on me, if he thought I was ugly and if he hated teaching me. I wanted him to answer that he would never give up on me, that he thought I was beautiful and that he loved teaching me.

As I lay there, I realized that throughout my entire life I had been careful not to shine too much. I had grown up believing that shining too much made other people feel bad. I had spent my life trying to be less so others could be more. It dawned on me that it wasn't working and I was exhausted from the efforts to be "less."

But I had been "less" for so long that it was now the path of least resistance. Allowing myself to be all that I could be—to be all that I am—seemed impossible. Maybe it was too late.

I wondered whether the butterfly ever doubted her ability to break free ...

FINDING MY CENTRE

"Find your centre and dance from it," he would say to me. I finally confessed I had no idea where my centre was or how to find it. He held my hands in his and asked me to close my eyes. He asked me to imagine that I was riding my horse and asked me where my centre was. I was struck by how hard he tried to find a helpful way to teach me.

I opened my eyes and told him I liked the way he tried so hard. He blushed and thanked me. I closed my eyes again but continued to struggle with the search for my centre. He asked me where my awareness was, where I received information and where my movements emanated from. That was easy. I pointed to a place just below my belly button.

"That explains everything," he said. "You have been dancing from the waist down. Your centre for dance needs to be higher."

While my eyes were still closed he asked me to imagine my centre rising up my body until it reached a place just below where my ribcage met. I felt it and began to turn from side to side, my new centre leading the movement. Everything else followed naturally.

I could imagine the possibilities. I could imagine how dance might feel coming from my centre. I felt balanced and whole and strong.

THE FIRST TEST

I did not want to take the test. I felt as if my entire life had been about meeting standards imposed on me by others. Finally I was doing something just for me and didn't care what anyone else thought or felt. I was not dancing to make anyone else happy; I was not dancing to impress anyone; I was not dancing to reach any particular level of competence; and I was not dancing to compete. I was dancing for me. I wanted to measure my progress in ounces of joy and moments of freedom, *not* on a scale of 1 to 100.

I was furious at my dance instructor for imposing this test on me. I tried to explain why I didn't want to take this test—why I didn't want to take any test—but he refused to listen. I could not understand why he was so insistent. We had reached an impasse. He told me that he was going to set up the test without telling me when, so that when I came in for one of my lessons I would be tested. I was left with the choice of taking the test against my will or walking out of the test and feeling embarrassed in front of the examiner.

I chose to proceed with the test. When it was over, I hated my dance instructor and hated dance. I didn't even care whether I ever danced again. Dance had lost its meaning for me.

I had let this man who had given me dance take it away from me.

I recognized that my dance instructor was human and that he wasn't going to get it right all of the time. I was disappointed, but I was able to forgive him. I was having more trouble forgiving myself for taking the test even when I had known deep down that it was wrong for me.

It was weeks before I went to the dance studio again. A big part of me was ready to walk away from dance. A smaller part of me was determined to reclaim dance for myself—to make it mine in a way that no one could ever take it from me again.

In my next lesson, we faced each other in a bit of a stand-off. I broke the silence and said to him that I was tired of this debate about testing and that I was frustrated at not being heard.

He looked up and away from me and was silent for a long time. When he spoke, there was nothing defensive or competitive left in his eyes. He said that he would trust me. He said he did not know how to teach outside the framework of testing but that he was willing to learn and would need my help.

I stood there, filled with gratitude and new respect for this man who was vulnerable enough to admit that he did not know how to give me what I needed, caring enough to be willing to learn and humble enough to ask for help.

All I could say was, "Thank you; it means a lot to me."

Dance was mine in a way that it had never been before. It was in almost losing dance that I truly found it, and it was in having to fight for it that it became mine.

THE POWER OF MY CENTRE

We were standing, poised to dance, and as I waited for him to begin I realized he was searching for his centre. I decided to do the same. Suddenly I was intensely aware of a place of strength and beauty right inside me. It was my centre. As I turned my energy and attention inward, I felt a place inside me growing and expanding. A quiet strength and warm energy flowed from my centre throughout my entire body. I was aware of being mentally, emotionally and sexually aroused. It felt absolutely wonderful.

Time slowed, and I was surprised when he asked me if I was ready to dance. I smiled and nodded and told him I had found my centre. He nodded with a look that said he already knew. When we began to dance, I moved from my centre. I felt the dance in my body and followed his lead without hesitation. I was completely connected to my body. As he dipped me, my body dropped slowly in complete control and as I rose again, I rose slowly, lifting from my centre. I felt a physical and emotional strength I had never known.

In the days that followed, if I stood with my eyes closed and breathed deeply, I could come back to that feeling.

BEING A SPECTATOR

I had watched the dance competition the week before, and when I arrived for my next lesson, he asked me how I had felt watching the competition. I hesitated, not quite sure how I had felt. I heard myself say, "I guess part of me was hoping that maybe someday I could do that."

He then asked what I meant by that. I didn't say anything but could feel the tears surfacing. After a long pause, he asked, "Do you mean that maybe someday you could be that beautiful and graceful?"

The tears began. And then he began to pour his love into me. He said he thought I was beautiful—no, he *knew* I was beautiful. He said he would do anything to help me feel as beautiful as he knew me to be.

He told me I needed to put it out there, that I needed to dance in a competition and that I not only needed to feel beautiful but also needed to feel beautiful in front of an audience. He promised he would train me until I was more than ready. He promised I would find the most beautiful gown—a gown that made me feel like Cinderella—and that I would wear sparkles and would feel beautiful and would dance beautifully.

And then he smiled and said, "I am not dancing you beautiful; you are. I'm just helping you see it."

He was right. I was dancing myself beautiful.

THE COMPETITION

The big day had finally arrived. I had worked hard. I had danced three or four nights a week. I had focused on the technique of each dance. I understood the need to land on the inside edge of my foot and to roll over onto the ball of my foot in the Latin movement. I had practised this until the inside edge of my foot had become one big callous. I understood the Latin hip motion and how it initiates on the floor and moves up from there. I had rolled my hips in so many figures of eight I worried that I might just roll out of bed in my sleep! I had focused on my frame in my smooth dances and stretched left as often as I could think of it. I had surrendered to all the feelings that flowed through me in that outward and upward position. I was ready to go out there. I was ready for my rite of passage.

I had struggled with my conflicted feelings about the importance of this competition. My head said, "It's no big deal," but my heart whispered, "It's a huge deal." I chose to listen to the whisper of my heart. I had to choose and re-choose to let it be as big a deal as it felt. I stopped minimizing and mocking it when I told people that I was going into a competition. I stopped saying, "What a joke," and "Can you believe it?" and started saying, "This is really important to me."

I arrived in Niagara Falls the night before the competition. I walked into the empty ballroom, and my heart sped up and my legs started shaking. My breath caught. I sat down. I breathed. I tried to imagine being on the dance floor the next day with judges and spectators watching. I felt the panic rising. I reminded myself that most of the spectators would be people from my dance studio, people I knew, people who cared about me. I breathed.

I went up and sat in one of the judge's chairs and tried to demystify their presence. The judges were simply people, people who may even remember what it was like to learn to dance.

I thought of myself earlier in the day when I had appeared in court dressed in my robes and confidently argued my client's case. I thought of the judge telling me to sit down and my refusal to sit down and my repeated demands for the court's indulgence to hear me out. Where was that confident lawyer now? I smiled at the idea that today I had been standing in court dressed in black and covered up from head to toe, and tomorrow I would be dancing across the floor in a little black dress. If they could see me now ...

Finally, I allowed myself to walk across the dance floor and feel it under my feet. I even did a single turn and smiled to myself. For better or for worse, I was ready. I had a long way to go in dance and had lots to learn and to improve upon, but for my first competition, I was ready. I turned and took one last look at the room and said goodnight to it.

I awoke the next morning feeling excited. It was like Christmas morning. Today was the day I would put on a pretty dress, put my hair up, put sparkly makeup on and go out there and dance.

I met my instructor on the dance floor for a quick warm-up. Ah, this wasn't so bad. I wasn't so nervous. My knees weren't shaking. Maybe this was going to be okay. The start time approached. Before I knew it, I was on deck. I listened to the waltz music playing and tried to feel it in my body.

And then it was my turn. My instructor arrived and took my hand and led me out on the dance floor. This was it. This was the much feared and much anticipated moment. This was the moment in which I would spread my wings and fly. I took a deep, slow breath. The music started, and we began to dance. I could feel the dance flow through me, stiffly at first and then more smoothly. I could feel the stretch. I could feel my centre. I could feel the connection with my dance instructor. This wasn't so bad after all.

I danced my first six dances back to back—novice waltz, tango, foxtrot, intermediate waltz, tango, foxtrot. I was grateful that things were not a blur. Time slowed down, and I was in the moment. And then it was over.

The award presentations began. I stood beside my dance instructor waiting to find out my placing. I reminded myself that it wasn't about coming first—it was about putting it out there. It was about having danced through my fear. And then I heard my name being called in first place. I had won. I tried to contain the feeling. I was surprised at just how good it felt. I glanced up at my dance instructor and caught his eye, and a warm glow of pride flooded through me.

There was a long wait before the Latin dances began. I changed into my little black dress and grew increasingly nervous. There was an expectation now that had not existed in the morning. I had come in first in the smooth dances, and maybe I could come in first in the Latin dances. I tried to be quiet and still. I tried to move around and just stay "in my body." But I felt myself drifting away. I felt myself retreating and shutting down.

I found myself on deck once again. But this time I was terrified. The music began, and I froze. I could not feel the music at all. I was terrified of not knowing where to go. I didn't even remember how to follow. This was awful. I wanted to run away.

And then it happened. My worst fear. I went the wrong way in the rumba. I ended up on the wrong foot, completely out of time with the music. I felt horrible. I didn't want to be out there anymore. I just wanted the song to end. In fact, I wanted the whole day to be over. This whole thing was so stupid. What was I doing out here? I was overwhelmed with shame, not just at my mistake, but at being here at all. I looked up at my instructor with a weak smile, and he suggested I do a turn. I did a feeble turn and somehow ended up back on the right foot, and the song finally ended.

I walked off the dance floor in utter defeat. I turned to my friend who had come with me for moral support and said, "Help me." She saw the look of defeat, hopelessness and panic in my eyes. Her strength and calmness seemed to grow in direct proportion to my terror. There was only one or two minutes before I had to go back out again.

I heard my name being called, and I breathed into every part of me and stood tall and took my dance instructor's arm and walked back out onto the dance floor. I gave as much of me as I could. I was relieved and proud that I had managed to pull myself back from my shame. I danced the rest of the Latin dances in a blur. I was simply going through the motions. I tried to give it my all in the last two dances, but I was tired. I was ready to go home.

The award presentations began. I stood breathless, hoping against all odds that I had come in first. And then I heard my name being called in last place. I had not come in first; I had lost. I felt such disappointment. I tried to minimize it. I smiled graciously on the outside while I shook with disappointment and shame on the inside. I saw the disappointment in my instructor's eyes and felt shame at having let him down. I was very tired.

STIRRING THINGS UP

When I arrived home that night, I watched the video and for the first time saw myself dance. I looked so young. I looked like a gawky teenager. I was a 34-year-old woman, and I looked like a teenager. I did not like what I saw.

I had a choice. I could acknowledge defeat and give up, or I could get angry and fight back. For several days, I wallowed in despair and hopelessness. I readied myself to return to a life of limitations. I prepared to give up my dream of flying. I grieved. I wasn't sure if I wanted to dance again.

I told my instructor I didn't think I was going to be able to access my aggression or my intensity or my passion or whatever the hell I was supposed to be accessing through dance. What I thought, but didn't say, was that maybe I didn't have any intensity or passion to access.

And so I went through the motions. I danced an hour here and an hour there.

And then I got angry—really, really angry. A fierce determination was growing inside me. A sense of entitlement was building. I had a right to my passion. I had a right to fly. God damn these restraints. God damn these restrictions. God damn the fear and the shame. I started imagining the possibilities. What if I stopped holding back? I breathed. What if I let myself fly? I struggled to breathe.

I began walking with my chest out and my head held high. I forced the breath, violently at times. I made tough choices. I decided to really show up in the first five minutes of my dance lesson, rather than waiting until the last five minutes. I gave myself permission to really try, to put it out there, to give it my all. I pushed and shoved and forced my way through the limitations and restrictions that were suffocating me.

I started running fast and flapping my wings. I was going to fly if it killed me.

THE TANGO (FOR REAL)

I was scheduled to perform a demonstration at the Graduation Ball. I thought I was going to be on the floor with three or four other couples, but minutes before I was to dance, I discovered I was doing a solo demonstration. At first I panicked. I didn't want to be out there by myself. And then I was just irritated at being nervous. I wanted to fly. I decided I would really go wherever I was led, and if I went in the wrong direction, at least I would go there with gusto. There was going to be nothing halfhearted about this dance. I would go all the way.

I looked at the dance floor and claimed it as my own—my universe, my dance floor. I laughed as I thought, *Hurry up and get off my dance floor—the woman in me is about to dance, and she's getting impatient!*

We walked onto the dance floor, and I took in the applause. I breathed it in. I stood 10 feet from my instructor and waited. The music began, and his hand went out. I walked into him and placed myself in tango position. We began to dance. I moved with strength and power. I felt it and knew he could too. His lead became more aggressive, more violent, and my follow became more intense, more passionate. My hair whipped across my face and covered my eyes as I stood motionless in a pause. I couldn't move my hair. My frame was solid. To move would be to destroy the dance. There was a sense of wild abandonment in leaving my hair covering my face. At the next turn, my hair whipped the other way and was out of my face. I felt free. The woman in me had been released.

The dance floor was barely big enough to contain my dance. My dance filled the room. I became the dance as I allowed myself to flow from my centre and dance from my soul.

When the music stopped and the dance finished, I was breathless with excitement. I could have danced all night. I could have stood in the applause all night. I left the dance floor and received accolades from the other students. It felt wonderful.

I was on fire.

I had found my passion.

I had danced myself beautiful.

ACKNOWLEDGEMENTS

I'd like to thank my parents for their constant love and support and my son for making every day beautiful.

I'd like to thank Andrew Bee, my first dance teacher, who danced me beautiful, and Arthur Baird, my current dance teacher, who quietly dances joy into my life every lesson.

A big thank you to my girlfriends, Deanna, Felicia and Helen, who each dance to the beat of their own hearts and live their lives to the fullest and to Neil for being one of the first *Dance Me Beautiful* fans and keeping the original copy in his toolbox all these years.

I'd like to thank Cameron and Lori, who hold the fort down at the office while I am dancing or writing.

Thank you to Arron and Kelley at Infinity Media Services Inc. for supporting me on the website and 'tech' side of things.

I'd like to thank the collaborative professionals I work with who dance peacefully in the midst of conflict, especially Victoria, Sheila, Laurie, Cori, Nicola, Jacqueline, Judith, Jane, Stella and Sharyn. I'd also like to thank Pam and Barbara for being role models in following their deepest passions while raising children and running their busy collaborative practices.

I'd like to thank the folks at Strategic Coach, whose workshops have kept me accountable to my life goals and given me the strategies to achieve them, and a special thank you to Patti, Tanya and the "A Team."

I'd like to thank everyone at iUniverse who believed in this book from the beginning and who helped make my dream come true.

And finally, I'd like to thank Brene Brown for her inspiring work on vulnerability, courage and authenticity. Her work and her books inspired me to share *Dance Me Beautiful*.

Printed in the United States
By Bookmasters